Where Animals Live

The World of a Jellyfish

Text by David Shale
and Jennifer Coldrey

Photographs by
Oxford Scientific Films

Gareth Stevens Publishing
Milwaukee

A Kind of Jellyfish —
and Where to Find It

The ocean is a large *habitat.* In *tropical* waters, the surface is often dotted with unusual objects. These objects look like small blue plastic bags filled with air. Each bag is called a float. The float, with its crest or sail on top, is part of a kind of jellyfish.

This animal is called a Portuguese Man-of-War. It is called this because its float looks like the sail of a boat.

lateen sail

This boat is called a Portuguese caravel, and its sail is called a "lateen sail."

The Man-of-War lives among the *plankton* in warm seas. The plankton is a mass of tiny plants and animals that floats near the ocean surface. Sometimes winds and ocean currents carry Men-of-War to the beach. As the animal dries out in the sun, its float and crest slowly collapse.

What Kind of Animal Is the Portuguese Man-of-War?

The Man-of-War is related to true jellyfish and other sea jellies. Together, they make up a group called *coelenterates*. This name means "hollow guts."

Each animal in this group is like a bag with a mouth at one end. Food passes in through the mouth, and food remains pass out through the mouth. Tentacles surround the mouth and push food into it.

Coelenterates are very simple animals. They have a simple nervous system, no brain, and no skeleton. They also have no heart or blood vessels. They breathe by absorbing oxygen from the water.

The simplest type of coelenterate is called a *polyp*. The Man-of-War is a more complicated type.

Many coelenterates, including the true jellyfish and the Man-of-War, float in the water. The Man-of-War is a special kind of sea jelly. We see only its float above the water. Most of the animal hangs below. It has long tentacles and stinging cells, or *nematocysts,* for catching *prey.*

The Floating Commune

The Portuguese Man-of-War is not like other sea jellies. It is not just one animal! It is a group of animals called a commune, or colony. The commune is made up of many polyps. All the polyps are linked. They work together as if they were one animal.

Four different kinds of polyp make up the Man-of-War. The float is the first kind. Some floats can be as big as 12 inches long and 6 inches high. The float is filled with air.

The float keeps the Man-of-War bobbing on the surface of the sea. Its crest acts as a sail. The other polyps hang down from the float into the water.

The tentacles are the second type of polyp. They can be from 10 to 100 feet long. The Man-of-War uses its tentacles to haul food up to its many mouths. An adult Man-of-War has seven main tentacles and many smaller ones. Thousands of nematocysts are on each tentacle.

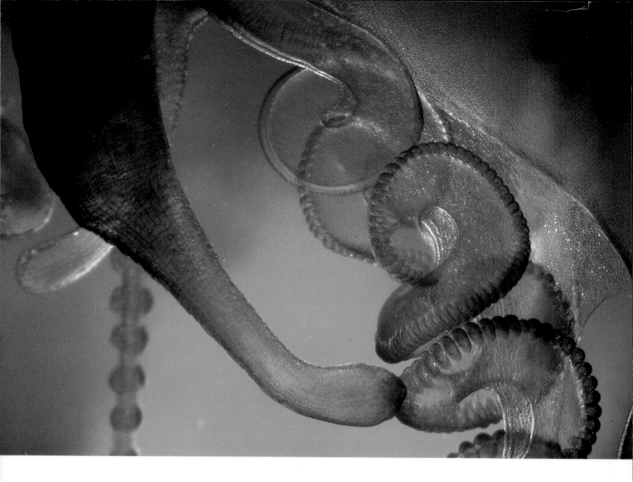

More Polyps in the Commune

The third kind of polyps are the stomach polyps.
There are many of these, and each has a mouth
at one end. They take the food from the tentacles
and digest it.

The fourth type of polyps are the reproductive
parts of the Man-of-War commune.

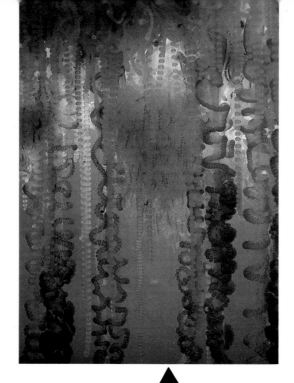

The reproductive parts hang in clusters among the tentacles. Scientists think that young Men-of-War grow from *fertilized* eggs. These eggs are shed by the female and fertilized by the male. The baby float polyp is the start of the entire commune. As the Man-of-War grows, other parts start to form. The smallest Men-of-War are less than $\frac{1}{10}$ inch long. See the difference between a very young and an older Man-of-War. The baby is about two inches long.

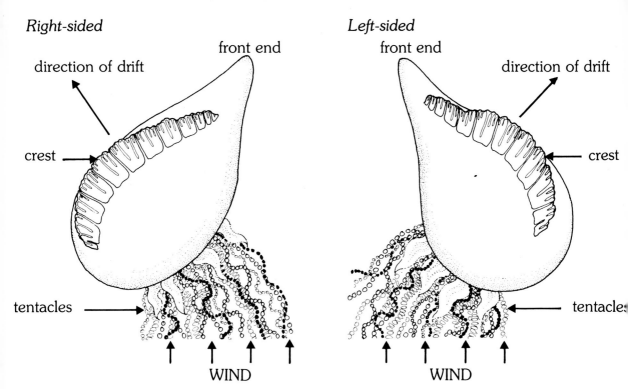

Right-sided

front end

direction of drift

crest

tentacles

WIND

Left-sided

front end

direction of drift

crest

tentacles

WIND

Floating and Sailing with the Wind

A Portuguese Man-of-War cannot swim. It can only drift and float wherever the wind and currents take it. It has no control over its speed or direction. The wind can blow the animal along at a little over one mile per hour.

The Man-of-War has a special *gland* at the base of the float. This gland controls the amount of air in the crest, or sail. And the amount of air controls how much the float is affected by the wind.

From time to time the float flops over and dips in the water. This tilting helps keep the float moist in calm water.

Men-of-War are lopsided. Most of their tentacles hang down from one side of the body, usually the *windward* side. A right-sided Man-of-War drifts to the left of the wind blowing across it. A left-sided Man-of-War drifts to the right of the wind. This difference in drift helps to spread these animals evenly over the seas.

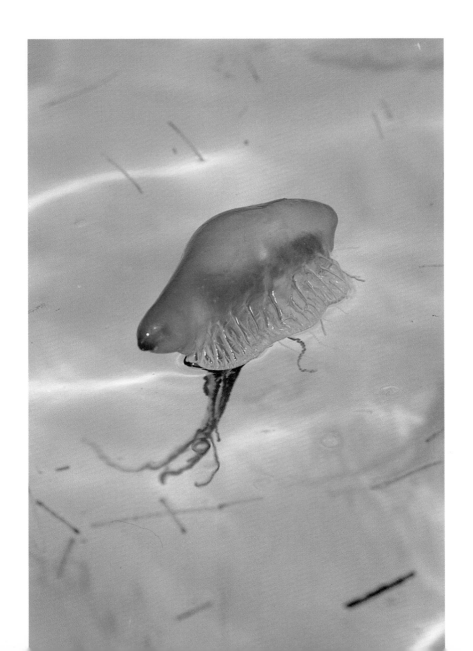

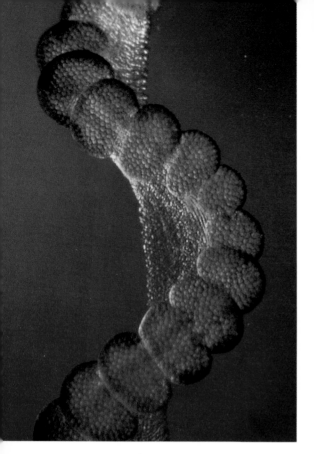

Poisonous Tentacles

The Man-of-War is a *predator*. Each tentacle is armed with thousands of stinging cells, or nematocysts. The nematocysts are in bands.

Each nematocyst is like a tiny hypodermic needle coiled up inside a cell. If another animal touches a tentacle, the stinging cells nearby are triggered off. Each cell explodes, and out shoots a hollow thread with a needle-sharp tip. The tip sticks into the animal. Poison travels down the thread and into the animal.

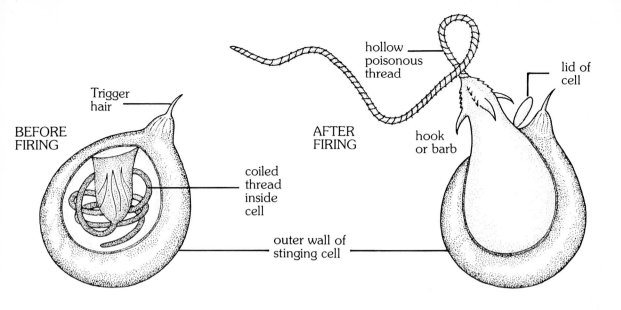

BEFORE
FIRING

Trigger
hair

hollow
poisonous
thread

lid of
cell

AFTER
FIRING

hook
or barb

coiled
thread
inside
cell

outer wall of
stinging cell

The poison can paralyze a fish in a few seconds. It can also cause great pain to people. Brushing against a tentacle can cause a burning or stinging feeling. A sting on the hand will send pain up the arm. A sting on the foot will send pain up the leg. Small stings go away in a few hours. Bad stings can hurt for weeks. Luckily, people rarely meet up with Men-of-War.

Catching Food

The Man-of-War's tentacles are quite long. An uncoiled tentacle can be 70 times as long as one that is coiled up. As the Man-of-War drifts, its tentacles are ready to trap fish. When a fish touches the tentacles, it is hooked and poisoned, all at once. The tentacles pull the prey up to the many stomach polyps. Each tentacle can work by itself. While one is hauling in its catch, others are fishing for more prey.

Each mouth of the Man-of-War is only about
$\frac{1}{25}$ inch wide when resting. When it is feeding,
however, it can stretch to more than $\frac{3}{4}$ inch wide.

Sometimes prey are small enough to be
swallowed whole. Other times the Man-of-War
will trap and eat large fish. Then many stomach
polyps attach themselves to the fish. Together
they cover the whole fish. They release juices
that break down the fish. Bit by bit, the food is
absorbed into the rest of the colony. Any remains
are pushed back out through the mouths of the
stomach polyps.

Large Enemies of the
Portuguese Man-of-War

The Man-of-War is poisonous and deadly to other animals. Yet *it* has enemies, too. The largest is the Ocean Sunfish. This giant fish weighs about 1100 lb. It may be as much as 10 feet long.

Two turtles, the Loggerhead (below) and the Hawksbill, also eat Men-of-War.

The Loggerhead has been seen trailing tentacles like strings of spaghetti. It shuts its eyes to protect them from the stings.

These animals don't seem to be harmed by the stings. There is even one octopus that breaks off the tentacles. It uses them to kill *its* prey.

Humans are not predators of the Man-of-War. But we harm them when we pollute their habitat with chemicals and oil spills.

Wind and waves also cause the death of many Men-of-War. This crab is feeding on a Man-of-War washed up on a beach in Bermuda. ↓

Small Enemies of the
Portuguese Man-of-War

Many small creatures also feed on the Portuguese Man-of-War. One of these is the Violet Sea Snail. Its shell is just over ⅝ inch long. It makes bubbles by trapping air in a *mucus* made from its foot. The mucus hardens around the bubbles. The snail then clings to these bubbles at the surface of the sea. This snail rasps away at the Man-of-War with its tongue. And it suffers no bad effects from the tentacles.

Another small enemy of the Man-of-War is a sea slug called *Glaucus*. This slug lives upside down just under the surface of the water. It is kept afloat by a bubble of air in its stomach. *Glaucus* eats any part of the Man-of-War it can reach. It even absorbs the unexploded stinging cells. It uses them later against other sea animals. Here the sea slug nibbles at the tentacles of a Man-of-War. With its feathery limbs, *Glaucus* looks quite different from its cousin, the sea snail.

The Friendly Clownfish

The Man-of-War is avoided by most sea
creatures. Some, however, can live with the Man-
of-War without getting stung. One, called a
yellow-jack, does so only when it is young. One
fish seems to like living among the Man-of-War's
tentacles all the time. That fish is the little
clownfish, often called the Man-of-War Fish. The
clownfish is only three inches long. Its speckled,
streaked body gives it *camouflage* as it swims
among the tentacles (above.) The stinging
tentacles themselves also protect the clownfish
from larger fish.

The clownfish is covered with a mucus film. This keeps the Man-of-War's nematocysts from firing. If the clownfish is hurt, the film will be broken, and the fish may end up as the Man-of-War's next meal!

As you know, the Man-of-War has many relatives, including sea anemones and jellyfish. Other clownfish live among the stinging tentacles of these animals. Here, a clownfish lives among the tentacles of a large sea anemone.

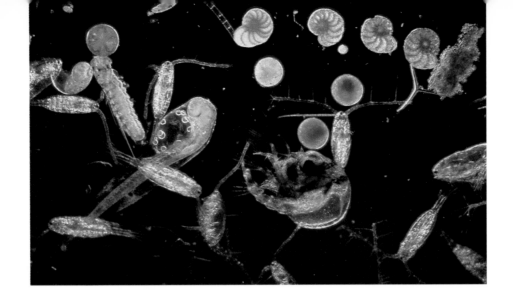

The World of Plankton

In the ocean, plants can grow only where light can reach them. That is why billions of tiny plants float near the ocean surface. These plants make up an important part of the plankton. They provide food to animals like these baby fish. These fish also make up part of the plankton — the animal plankton.

← The plankton also includes billions of tiny animals, *eggs*, and *larvae*. This drop of seawater (left) is home to small shrimps, a baby crab, and a fish larva. They can be seen only under a microscope.

The animal plankton also includes larger animals. Unlike plants, animals don't need sunlight for food. After feeding at night, many animals sink back to deeper water. There, underwater currents carry them to new parts of the ocean.

Larger animals like the Man-of-War stay near the surface. Here is a young Man-of-War with its tiny float and tentacles. It is surrounded by two white shells and some sea jellies called *Porpitas*.

↓

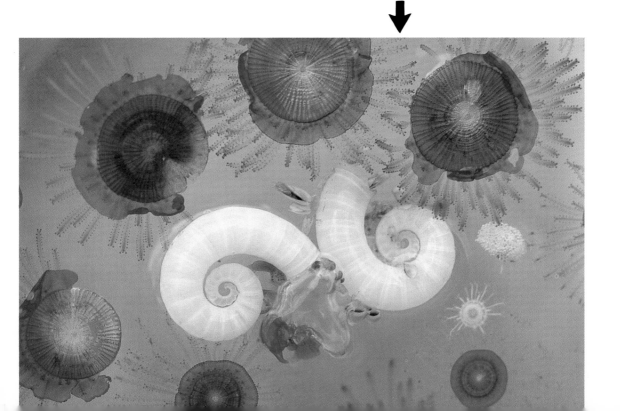

More Floating Jellies

Many other types of sea jellies float at or just below the ocean surface. One is called Jack Sail-by-the-Wind. It is like the Man-of-War in some ways.

Its float is much smaller (one inch long) than that of the Man-of-War, and it has several air chambers. Beneath the float hangs one stomach polyp with a big mouth. This is surrounded by reproductive polyps and a ring of short tentacles. Like the Man-of-War, these animals are either right-sided or left-sided. They often cruise the seas by the thousands.

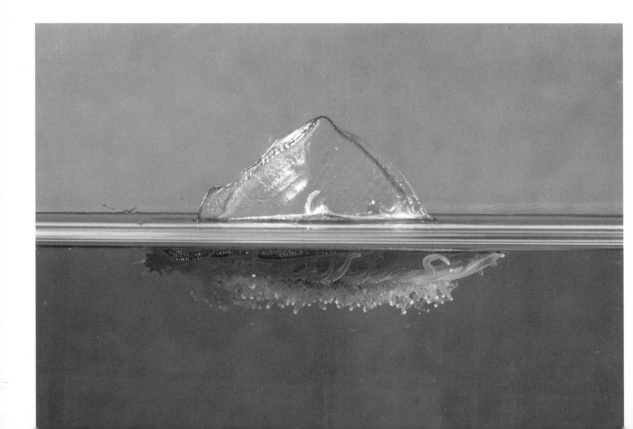

↑

Another tiny sea jelly found near the surface is the *Porpita*. This picture was taken from above. As it shows, *Porpitas* have circular floats. They have no sail, however, and are only one inch wide.

This is what *Porpita* looks like below the surface. The stiff tentacles stick out from the edge of the float, like wheel spokes. The stinging cells are in knobs on the tentacles.

↓

Swimming Jellies

There are many kinds of jellyfish. True jellyfish
are swimmers. They do not rely on the currents
alone to move around. Like all true jellyfish, this
Lion's Mane Jellyfish swims or floats below
the surface.

Jellyfish come in all sizes. Some are as small as a
pea. Others are larger than a dinner plate. One
giant jellyfish from the Arctic can be more than
seven feet across.

The true jellyfish is shaped like a bell or an umbrella. It swims by opening and closing its umbrella. Unlike the Man-of-War, true jellyfish are made up of one body, not several polyps.

Comb jellies are another group of sea jellies. Their *luminescent* bodies glow in the dark. Their comb-like plates beat and propel them through the water. Comb jellies catch their prey with sticky tentacles. Many are no bigger than a pea.

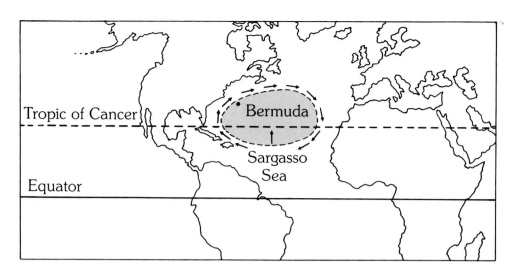

Tropic of Cancer

Bermuda

Sargasso
Sea

Equator

The Seaweed Sea ⬆

One place where you can find the Man-of-War is
the Sargasso Sea. It is part of the Atlantic Ocean.
It lies east of North America and north of the
West Indies. It was first sighted by Christopher
Columbus in 1492. Its size is about half that of
Europe. Floating on the surface of this sea is a
huge mass of seaweed. This seaweed is called
Sargassum Weed. ⬇

← Swift ocean currents surround the Sargasso Sea. Inside the loop of these currents, however, the water is calmer — and about three feet higher — than the surrounding ocean. The calm seas help many animals survive in the Sargassum Weed. These animals include sea anemones, crabs, shrimps, sponges, sea slugs, and fish.

The Man-of-War and other sea jellies can also be found here. Sometimes the Man-of-War becomes tangled in the seaweed. There, it becomes easy prey for such enemies as the Violet Sea Snail, *Glaucus*, and any crabs (below) that live in the weed.

↓

Life on the Ocean Surface

The ocean surface is an ever-changing habitat. Some areas are rich in life. Others are empty. These areas change with the currents. The Man-of-War lives in this changing world. Its trailing tentacles net it more than enough food, however. And in turn, other animals feed on the Man-of-War. In this way, food and energy are passed on from plants through animals.

Food Chain

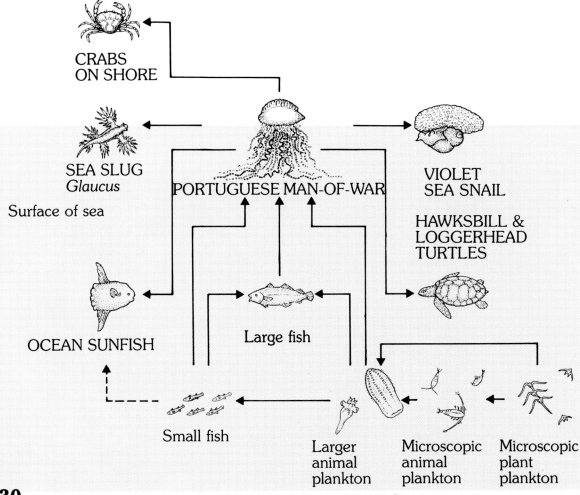

CRABS
ON SHORE

SEA SLUG
Glaucus

Surface of sea

PORTUGUESE MAN-OF-WAR

VIOLET
SEA SNAIL

HAWKSBILL &
LOGGERHEAD
TURTLES

OCEAN SUNFISH

Large fish

Small fish

Larger
animal
plankton

Microscopic
animal
plankton

Microscopic
plant
plankton

The Man-of-War is well-adapted to its life on the seas. Thanks to its float and its weapons, it is protected against wind, waves, and predators. It has few enemies and should survive a long time as it wanders the open seas.

New Words About Jellyfish and the Portuguese Man-of-War

These new words about jellyfish and the Portuguese Man-of-War appear in the text on the pages shown after each definition. Each new word first appears in the text in *italics*, just as it appears here.

camouflage .....animal disguise; how animals hide by blending with their background. **20**

coelenterates ...(sih-LEN-ter-rates) a group of jelly-like animals, including sea anemones, corals, and jellyfish. **5**

fertilize(d) ....to join a male sperm cell with a female's egg, so that a new individual can grow from the fertilized egg. **9**

gland ....a part of the body that produces a special substance. **10**

habitat ....the natural home of an animal or plant. **2, 17, 30**

larvae ....young forms (after the egg stage) of many water animals. **23**

luminescent .....giving off light without heat. **27**

mucus ....slimy substance produced by some animals. **18, 21**

nematocysts ....stinging cells of a coelenterate. **5, 7, 12, 21**

plankton ....the mass of tiny animals and plants that drifts in the upper waters of the sea. **3, 22, 23**

polyp ....a simple, cylinder-shaped animal with a mouth at one end -- the simplest form of coelenterate. **5, 6, 8, 9, 14, 15, 24, 27**

predator ....an animal that kills and eats other animals. **12, 17, 31**

prey ....an animal that is killed and eaten by another animal. **5, 14, 15, 17, 27, 29**

tropical ....having to do with the warm regions of the Earth on either side of the Equator. **2**

windward ....side on which the wind blows. **11**

Reading level analysis: SPACHE 2.4, FRY 2, FLESCH 96 (very easy), RAYGOR 3, FOG 6, SMOG 3

Library of Congress Cataloging-in-Publication Data

Coldrey, Jennifer.
The world of a jellyfish.
(Where animals live)
Summary: Text and illustrations describe the physical characteristics, habits, and natural environment of the jellyfish.
1. Medusae -- Juvenile literature. [1. Jellyfishes] I. Shale, David. II. Oxford Scientific Films. III. Title. IV. Series.
QL377.S4C65 1986   593.7   86-5704

ISBN 1-55532-098-8
ISBN 1-55532-073-2 (lib. bdg.)

North American edition first published in 1987 by
Gareth Stevens, Inc.
7221 West Green Tree Road Milwaukee, Wisconsin 53223, USA
US edition, this format, copyright © 1987 by Belitha Press Ltd.
Text copyright © 1987 by Gareth Stevens, Inc.

First conceived, designed, and produced by Belitha Press Ltd., London, as **The Man-of-War at Sea,** with an original text copyright by Oxford Scientific Films. Format copyright by Belitha Press Ltd.

Typeset by Ries Graphics ltd., Milwaukee.
Printed in the United States of America.
Series Editor: Mark J. Sachner.
Art Director: Treld Bicknell. Line Drawings: Lorna Turpin.
Design: Naomi Games. Cover Design: Gary Moseley.
Scientific Consultants: Gwynne Vevers and David Saintsing.

The publishers wish to thank the following for permission to reproduce copyright material: **Oxford Scientific Films Ltd.** for pp. 1, 4, 6, 7, 8, 9 below, 11, 12 both, 13, 15, 18, 19, 20, 22 above, 23, 24, 25 both, 27, 29, 31 (photographer Peter Parks); pp. 2, 3 below, 9 above, 14, 21, and 26 (photographer David Shale); p. 16 above (photographer G. Merlen); p. 16 below (photographer Keith Gillett); p. 17 (photographer Sean Morris); p. 22 below (photographer Laurence Gould); p. 28; back cover (photographer Peter Parks). **Planet Earth Pictures** for front cover (photographer Andrew Mountner).

4 5 6 7 8 9 92 91 90 89